dabble lab

JUNIOR MAKERS

3D PEN
PROJECTS
FOR BEGINNERS

BY TAMMY ENZ

4D™

an Augmented
Reading
Experience

CONSULTANT:
Jessica Stewart
Dean of Library and
Academic Technology
The Meadows School
Las Vegas, Nevada

CAPSTONE PRESS
a capstone imprint

Dabble Lab is published by
Capstone Press, a Capstone imprint
1710 Roe Crest Drive
North Mankato, Minnesota 56003
www.mycapstone.com

Library of Congress Cataloging-in-Publication Data
Library of Congress Cataloging-in-Publication Data is available
on the Library of Congress website.

ISBN 978-1-5157-9489-9 (library binding)
ISBN 978-1-5157-9493-6 (eBook PDF)

• • • • • •

EDITOR
Mari Bolte

DESIGNER
Tracy McCabe

**STUDIO PROJECT
PRODUCTION**
Marcy Morin, Sarah Schuette

PRODUCTION
Katy LaVigne

• • • • • •

Image Credits
All photographs by Capstone Studio: Karon Dubke except
Shutterstock: Kalabi Yau, cover (top), ProstoSvet, cover (bottom),
Veja, 6, 7 (both); Illustrations by Dario Brizuela

Design Elements
Shutterstock: TairA

Printed and bound in the USA.
010759S18

TABLE OF CONTENTS

DRAW SOMETHING GREAT

Drawing with pen and paper is fun. But if you want to amp up art, a 3D pen is the way to go. A 3D pen works like a regular pen. But there's one major difference — it uses plastic filament instead of ink.

3D drawing allows you to create projects that really do jump off the page. Instead of using computers and mechanics to make 3D designs, these pens let users draw freehand. They can make fast, cheap models of designs. Artists, engineers, architects, jewelry makers, and other craftsmen and -women find them helpful.

You can create toys, jewelry, models, and more. Mix drawing with art supplies like beads and tissue paper for more options. Practice your skills, and then use what you learn to keep imagining.

Download the Capstone 4D app!

- Ask an adult to search in the Apple App Store or Google Play for "Capstone 4D".
- Click Install (Android) or Get, then Install (Apple).
- Open the app.
- Scan any of the following spreads with this icon:

When you scan a spread, you'll find fun extra stuff to go with this book! You can also find these things on the web at www.capstone4D.com using the password: makers.3D

Although 3D printing has been around for decades, 3D pens are a new invention. They were first used in 2013.

3D pens work a lot like hot glue guns. The pens heat special plastics, which can then be shaped or formed. Most pens use a plastic filament called PLA (poly-lactic acid) or ABS (acrylonitrile butadiene styrene). Newer professional-grade pens can use filament that contains wood, metal, or nylon.

TIP: Never touch the tip of the 3D pen. It gets very hot and can burn you.

WHY IT WORKS: PLA filament is made from things like cornstarch, sugar cane, and tapioca root. It is biodegradable and doesn't give off fumes. It also melts at a lower temperature. It's better for the environment than ABS, which is oil based. ABS is stronger and more flexible, though, and works better for wearable projects.

NAME CHAIN

Make a 2D drawing into a 3D chain that twists and moves. Practice writing, cutting, and fusing with this quick craft.

YOU'LL NEED:

pen and paper
waxed paper
scissors

DIRECTIONS:

1: With the pen and paper, draw your name in bubble letters. Each letter should be about 2 inches (5 centimeters) tall.

2: Place a piece of waxed paper over the letters. Trace each letter onto the waxed paper with the 3D pen. Make each letter a different color.

3: Carefully peel the letters off the waxed paper.

4: Use scissors to cut the edge of every other letter.

5: Link the letters to each other to make a chain.

6: Close the cut letters with a dot of filament.

7: To make a hanger for your chain, draw a large S shape with the 3D pen. Add an extra loop to one end of the S. Hook the chain onto the loopy end. Use the other end to hang the chain off a ledge.

TIP: Some letters, like A and O, have floating center pieces. Connect them to the edge of the letter with lines of filament.

WHY IT WORKS: Real chains are made by individual links fused together. Your name chain is built the same way

MODEL HOME

Engineers make models of buildings. The models can be made out of materials like metal or cardboard. Now engineers can use 3D pens and printers too. Try it out yourself!

YOU'LL NEED:

pencil and paper
ruler
waxed paper

DIRECTIONS:

For the blueprints:

1: Use the pencil to draw a square on the paper. The square's sides should all be 3.5-inches (9-cm)-long.

2: Draw a second square the same size. Add a peak by drawing a triangle 1.5 inches (4 cm) tall on top.

For the house:

3: Place the waxed paper over the squares. Trace them with the 3D pen. Color them in, if desired. Make four squares.

4: Trace the peaked triangle. Color it in, if desired. Then make a second triangle.

5: Line up a square with the bottom of one peaked piece. Attach them with filament. Repeat with another square and the second peaked piece.

6: Attach the pieces from step 5 to two squares, to make the four walls of the house.

7: Set two squares on top for the roof. Use filament to attach them.

2

4

5

TIP: Before connecting the pieces, add doors and windows. Fill in the walls and roof with filament to make them solid.

WHY IT WORKS: Engineers and architects draw 2D drawings of each part of a building. They can use these drawings to create the pieces to construct a 3D model. 3D models help architects show others their plans and ideas. Models can help them find flaws or think of better or different ideas.

PUZZLING
STUFF

Do you like to solve puzzles? Regular 2D puzzles make a 2D picture. But a 3D puzzle can actually create an object. Try making - and then building - one yourself.

YOU'LL NEED:

permanent marker
plastic egg
3 to 4 different colors of filament

STEPS:

1: Use the marker to draw 3 to 4 connecting shapes on the egg.

2: Carefully trace over one of these shapes with the 3D pen.

3: Draw back and forth to fill in the outline.

4: Let this shape harden for a minute. Then carefully pull it off the egg.

5: Repeat steps 2 through 4 to create the other pieces of the puzzle.

6: Give the pieces to a friend to put together. When the puzzle has been solved, fuse the pieces together. Connect the edges with small dots of filament.

WHY IT WORKS: 3D filament is pliable when warm. It forms to the shape of the surface it is placed on. This is useful in creating hollow objects, like this puzzle.

TIP: 3D puzzles offer an extra challenge for the mind! Try making larger puzzles and adding more pieces.

FUSED FLYER

Bring butterflies, moths, or dragonflies to life!
Find your favorite photos. Your 3D pen will do
the rest!

YOU'LL NEED:

waxed paper
photos or drawings of butterflies, moths, or other winged insects
filament the color of the insect's body
tissue paper
scissors

STEPS:

1: Place the waxed paper over the image of the insect.

2: With the 3D pen, trace and fill in the insect's body and antennae.
Quickly peel the pieces from the waxed paper. Bend
the insect's antennae upward while the plastic is still soft.
Set the body aside.

3: Replace the waxed paper with the tissue paper.
Trace the insect's wing. Then add details.

4: Use the scissors to cut around the outside of the wing.

5: Repeat step 3 to make another wing. It should be the mirror image
of the first wing.

6: Attach the wings to the body with small dots of filament. Fold the
wings in a little.

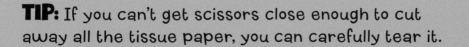

TIP: If you can't get scissors close enough to cut away all the tissue paper, you can carefully tear it.

WHY IT WORKS: Tissue paper is more absorbent than waxed paper or cardboard. This helps it fuse to the filament.

3D FIDGET
SPINNER

Like 3D pens, fidget spinners can be fun to play with! Get the best of both worlds when you make your own spinner out of filament.

YOU'LL NEED:

waxed paper
fidget spinner template
heavy-duty toothpick
pencil
penny
scissors

STEPS:

1: Place the waxed paper over the fidget spinner template of your choice. Trace the outline onto the waxed paper with the 3D pen.

2: Color in the spinner. Leave a small hole in the center. The toothpick should be able to pass through the hole.

3: Peel the spinner off the waxed paper. Fill in any bare spots with more filament.

4: Use the pencil to trace the penny onto the template paper. Remove the penny. Place waxed paper over the circle.

5: Trace over the circle with the 3D pen. Leave a small hole in the center. Repeat to make a second circle.

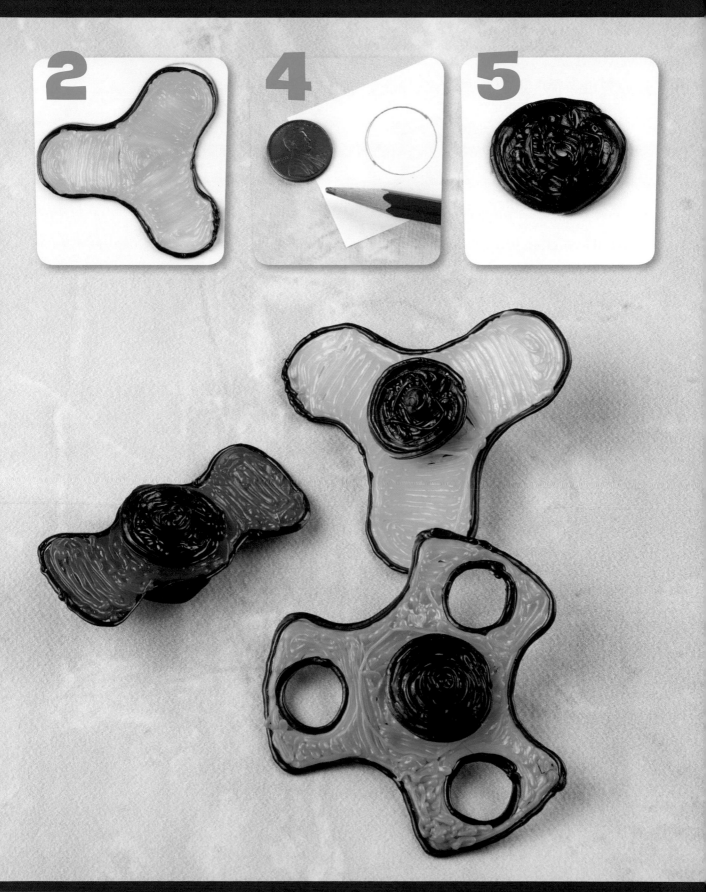

continued

6: Have an adult cut the toothpick into thirds. Set two pieces aside and use them for additional spinners. Fill in the center of one of the circles, and quickly push one end of the toothpick into the hot filament. Make sure the toothpick is straight. Press the end of the toothpick completely through the filament if you can.

7: Thread the spinner and second circle onto the toothpick. Add a large dab of filament to the end of the toothpick. Gently press the circle up so the filaments fuse together.

8: Keep adding filament to hold the toothpick firmly in place.

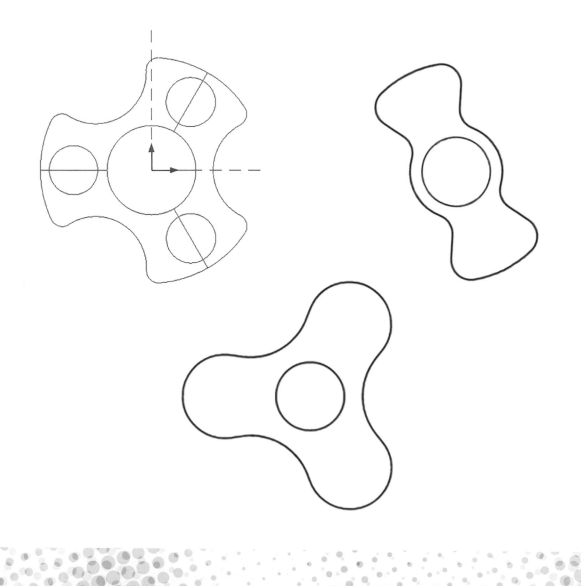

6

7

TIP: It might take a couple tries to make the perfect spinner. Don't give up!

WHY IT WORKS: Real fidget spinners use ball bearings to spin. This simpler version spins around the toothpick. But both use centripetal force to keep spinning.

TRANSLUCENT TISSUE

You can make larger projects without using huge amounts of filament! Build a base for a stained glass display. Then use tissue paper and your 3D pen to make something great.

YOU'LL NEED:

pencil
ruler
cardboard
several colors of tissue paper
scissors
black filament
suction cup with a hook

STEPS:

1: Trace a 5 inch (13 cm) square on the cardboard.

2: Draw a geometric pattern inside the square.

3: Cut pieces of tissue paper to fill in the design. Make the pieces a little larger than the shape they will fill.

4: Set the pieces inside the square. Their edges should overlap.

continued

5: Go over the square with black filament. The filament will fuse to the paper and connect the pieces.

6: Carefully trace your stained glass design with the pen.

7: Cut or tear away any extra tissue paper.

8: Use the 3D pen to make a loop in one corner of the square. Then slip the loop onto the suction cup's hook.

9: Show off your art by hanging it in a window.

TIP: You can make any shape or size stained glass once you get the hang of it.

WHY IT WORKS: Tissue paper is translucent, which means it lets some light shine through. Stained glass is also translucent. At the right time of day, the sun's rays will pass through as bands of color.

BEADED BRACELET

You can pair 3D pens with all sorts of craft supplies. Just like filament, plastic beads come in many colors. Mix and match both to make jewelry that fits your style.

YOU'LL NEED:

measuring tape
pencil
waxed paper
plastic beads

STEPS:

1: Use the measuring tape to figure out how long you want your bracelet.

2: Draw a line matching your measured length onto the waxed paper.

3: Flip the waxed paper over. Trace over the line with your 3D pen.

4: Make a 1/2-inch (1.5-cm) circle at one end. This is the toggle loop.

5: Make small O shapes with the 3D pen to make small beads. Use a variety of colors.

6: Thread the 3D beads onto bracelet. Alternate them with the plastic beads.

7: Draw a ¾-inch (2-cm) perpendicular line at the other end of the bracelet. This is the toggle bar.

8: To clasp the bracelet, slide the toggle bar through the loop.

TIP: Add a few dots of filament at the ends of the bracelet where they attach to the loop and toggle.

TIP: Make multicolor beads! Draw a circle as a template for 3D beads. Then make small dots around the circle. Switch filament colors, and fill in the spaces with dots of another color. You can also use regular plastic or pony beads if you don't want to make your own.

WHY IT WORKS: Toggle clasps are easy to make. They also make it easy to put on and take off your jewelry. Instead of a round loop, try squares, hearts, flowers, or other shapes.

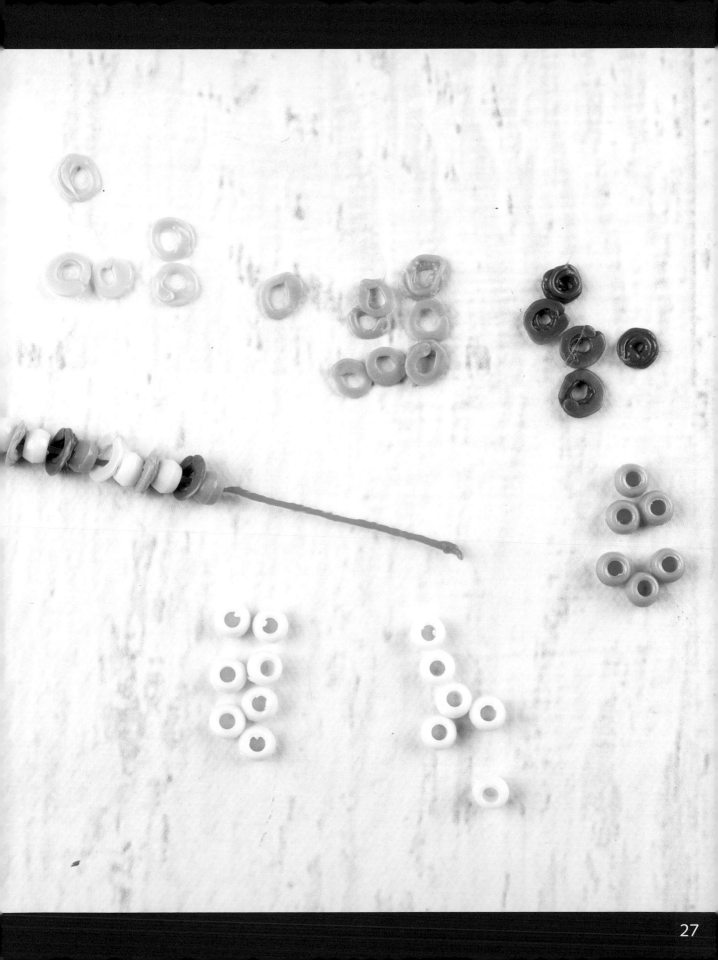

PALM TREE

Take a mini vacation! Many small pieces come together to make one large 3D tree.

YOU'LL NEED:

waxed paper
brown filament
templates
green filament

STEPS:

1: Place the waxed paper over the template image of the tree's trunk. Use the 3D pen to trace over the template with brown filament.

2: Repeat step 1 until you have four pieces. Set two pieces next to each other. Use filament to connect the pieces.

3: Connect the other two pieces to make the base. All four pieces should be facing a different direction.

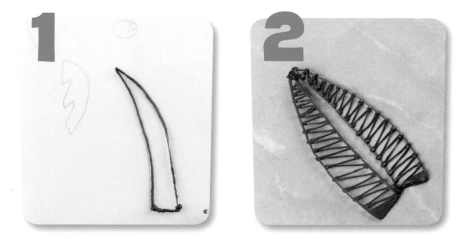

4: Place the waxed paper over the template image of the palm leaves. Use the 3D pen to trace over the template with green filament.

5: Repeat step 4 until you have at least 6 palm leaves.

6: Use filament to attach the leaves to the tree base. The leaves should fan out evenly around the tree.

7: Place the waxed paper over the template image of the coconuts. Use the 3D pen to trace over the template with brown filament and fill in each coconut. Add three small dots for eyes. Then attach the coconuts to the palm tree.

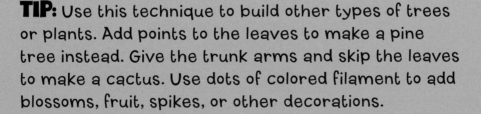

TIP: Use this technique to build other types of trees or plants. Add points to the leaves to make a pine tree instead. Give the trunk arms and skip the leaves to make a cactus. Use dots of colored filament to add blossoms, fruit, spikes, or other decorations.

WHY IT WORKS: By attaching the flat tree base pieces together, you've just turned a 2D object into a 3D object! Build up with the base, and then out with the leaves. Add more filament to make the tree trunk solid and round if you want. Then see how many leaves you can add!

HIDDEN PICTURE
CANDLE HOLDER

One of the coolest features of 3D pens is the ability to make 2D drawings into real things you can use. Turn hidden pictures into a candleholder. Your designs will dance off the walls!

YOU'LL NEED:

pencil and paper
ruler
waxed paper
battery-powered tea light

STEPS:

1: Draw an 8-inch (20-cm)-long line on the paper.

2: Make a 4-inch (10-cm) line at both ends of the 8-inch line.

3: Place waxed paper over the drawing.

4: Use the 3D pen to trace the lines onto the waxed paper. This will be the bottom and side seams for the candleholder.

5: Add a wavy line. It should start at the top of one 4-inch line and end at the other.

6: Draw pictures or words inside the lines.

7: Draw squiggly lines across the pictures to join them and add stability.

8: Carefully peel the drawing from the waxed paper.

9: Roll the drawing into a cylinder shape. The 4-inch lines should touch. Fuse them together.

10: Set the cylinder upright on a piece of paper. Draw around the cylinder to make the candle holder's base.

11: Place waxed paper over the base. Trace it with the 3D pen. Fill it in with shapes and squiggly lines.

12: Remove the base from the waxed paper. Attach it to the bottom of the cylinder with filament.

13: Place the tea light in the candleholder.

14: Turn the tea light on and the room lights off. You'll see your hidden pictures projected on the walls.

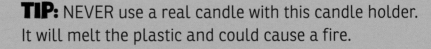

TIP: NEVER use a real candle with this candle holder. It will melt the plastic and could cause a fire.

WHY IT WORKS: Shadows are made when something solid blocks light. In this case, the pictures you drew are the solid thing. The tea light is the light. When the tea light is turned on, your drawings will be cast on the walls as shadows. Try making this using the tissue paper technique for some added color.

3D STAR

Small, identical pieces can be combined to make something larger. Use the skills you've mastered to turn 2D shapes into a bigger 3D object!

YOU'LL NEED:

waxed paper
2 different colors of filament
scissors

STEPS:

1: Place a sheet of waxed paper over the template. Use the 3D pen to trace the edges in one color.

2: Decorate the inside of the triangle with lines or squiggles. Peel the triangle from the waxed paper. Use scissors to clean up the edges.

3: Repeat steps 1 and 2 to make four more triangles.

4: Repeat steps 1 and 2 with a different color. Then make four more triangles.

5: Lay two triangles of different colors together on a flat surface. Make sure their long sides are touching.

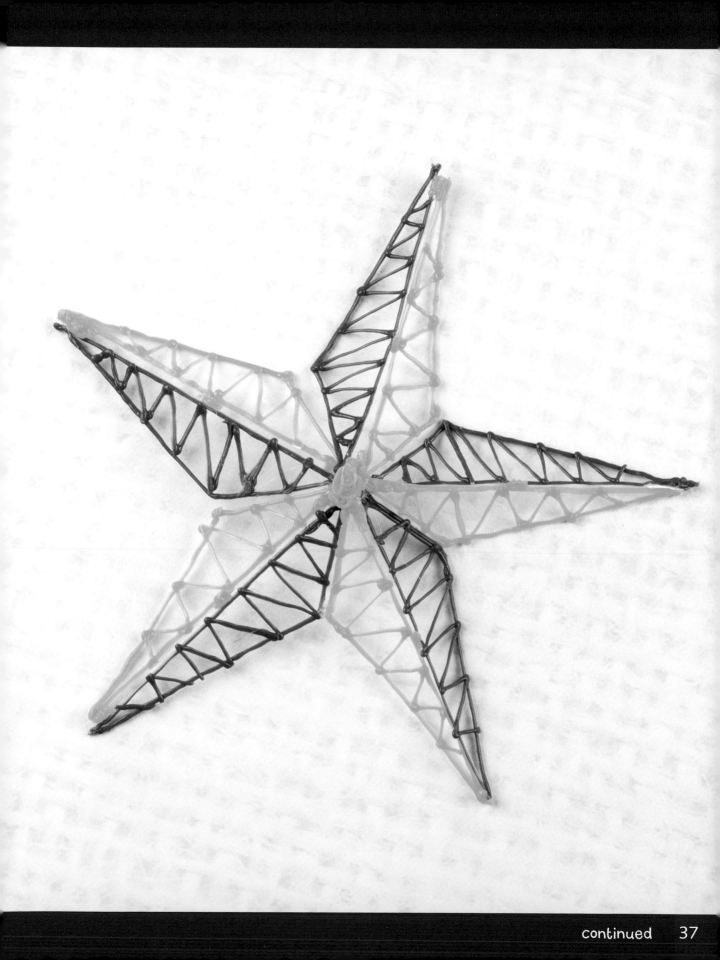

6: Use a dot of filament at each end and in the middle of these sides to join the triangles.

7: While the plastic is still warm, quickly fold the triangles to make a tent shape.

8: Repeat steps 5 through 7 to make four more tent shapes.

9: Line up the short points of each piece to form a star.

10: One piece at a time, use filament to join the points together at the tips. Reinforce the short sides of the pieces, if needed.

11: When the star is complete, finish it with a large dot of filament at its center.

TIP: Make another star. Fuse the bases of the two stars together. Now you have a two-sided 3D star.

WHY IT WORKS: Triangles and stars are symmetrical shapes. If you cut something symmetrical in half, both sides would be exactly the same. Both 2D and 3D shapes can have symmetry. For example, triangles are symmetrical. Their 3D shape, pyramids, are too. Other examples include squares and cubes.

Changing the shape of the triangle used will change the shape of this star. What happens when you make the sides longer or shorter? Your star might end up needing more or fewer points.

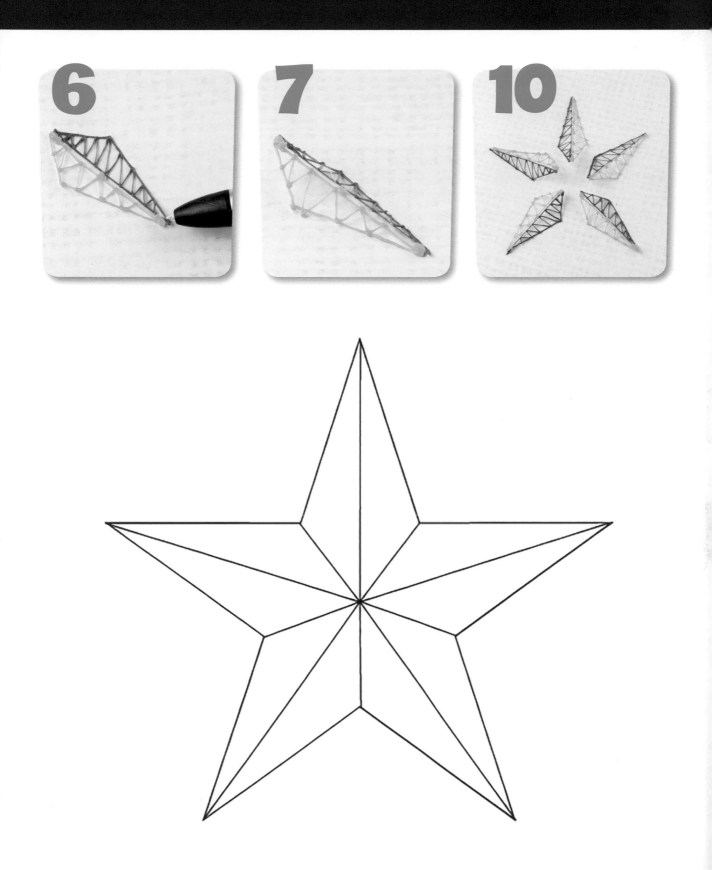

FAT CAT

This fat cat takes a little time to build. But once you make it, you'll be able to use the same steps to make other 3D animals too.

YOU'LL NEED:

modeling clay
clear tape
white filament
orange filament
black filament
pink filament
fishing line
scissors

STEPS:

1: Roll the clay into a small egg shape. It should be about half the size of a chicken egg.

2: Carefully wrap tape around the clay. Cover the clay completely.

3: Cover one half of the egg shape with white filament. This will be the cat's underside.

4: Set the white shape aside.

5: Cover the other half of the egg with orange filament. This will make the top of the cat.

6: Set the clay aside.

7: Hold the orange and white pieces together to form an egg shape. This is the cat's body. Use orange filament to glue the pieces together.

continued

8: Draw four orange legs on waxed paper. Each piece should be 0.75 by 0.25 inches (2 by 0.5 cm). Add several layers to add thickness.

9: Attach each leg to the orange part of the cat's body.

10: Make the tail the same way you made the legs. The tail should be about 3 inches (8 cm) long. Peel it off the waxed paper right away. Give it a slight curl.

11: Attach the tail to the cat.

12: Make the cat's neck next. Draw a small orange circle directly onto the body. Build layers to the circle until the neck is about 0.25 inches tall.

13: For the cat's head, roll a marble-sized piece of clay. Cover it with tape.

14: Use orange filament to cover half of the clay. Set the clay aside.

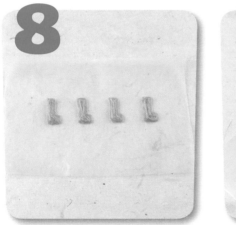

15: Place the orange piece on the cat's neck. Use orange filament to attach the head to the neck.

16: Carefully draw orange triangle-shaped ears on the head.

17: Use more orange to build a pointy nose on the cat's face.

18: Cover the cat's nose with white. Make a stripe on the cat's forehead.

19: Add a bit of white to tip of the tail.

20: Use black filament to draw two small eyes.

21: Cut three whiskers about 3 inches (8 cm) long from the fishing line.

22: Hold the centers of the whiskers to the end of the cat's nose. Attach them with a dot of pink filament.

TIP: Use a similar method to make other 3D creatures. Mice, dogs, horses, cows, pigs - you can make a whole barnyard!

WHY IT WORKS: Building a 3D animal can use a lot of filament. By using the clay, you can make a frame and save on building materials. The clay will also help keep pieces the same size, and make it easier to attach them later.

GLOSSARY

filament (FI-luh-muhnt)-a long, thin strip of plastic used with 3D pens

model (MOD-uhl)-something that is made to look like a person, animal, or object

perpendicular (PUR-puhn-DI-cu-luhr)-straight up and down relative to another surface; the two lines that form the letter T are perpendicular to each other

pliable (PLY-uh-buhl)-easily bent

project (pruh-JEKT)-to cause light to show on another surface

stability (STUH-bil-UH-tee)-adding or giving something to help an object resist forces and motion

template (TEM-plate)-a pattern used to trace or cut out shapes

READ MORE

Challoner, Jack. *Maker Lab: 28 Super Cool Projects: Build, Invent, Create, Discover.* New York: DK Publishing, 2016.

Holzweiss, Kristina. *I Can Make Remarkable Robots.* New York: Children's Press, an imprint of Scholastic Inc., 2018.

Sjonger, Rebecca. *Maker Projects for Kids Who Love Games.* New York: Crabtree Publishing Company, 2016.

MAKERSPACE TIPS

Download tips and tricks for using this book and others in a library makerspace.

Visit www.capstonepub.com/dabblelabresources

INTERNET SITES

Use FactHound to find Internet sites related to this book.

Visit www.facthound.com

Just type in 9781515794899 and go.

 Check out projects, games and lots more at
www.capstonekids.com

INDEX